OFFICE POLITICS
Positive Results from Fair Practices

Rebecca Luhn Wolfe, Ph.D.

A FIFTY-MINUTE™ SERIES BOOK

CRISP PUBLICATIONS, INC.
Menlo Park, California

OFFICE POLITICS
Positive Results from Fair Practices

Rebecca Luhn Wolfe, Ph.D.

CREDITS
Production Editor: **Karla Maree**
Editor: **Robert Racine**
Typesetting: **ExecuStaff**
Cover Design: **Carol Harris**
Artwork: **Ralph Mapson**

Copyright © 1997 by Crisp Publications, Inc.

Printed in the United States of America by Bawden Printing Company.

Distribution to the U.S. Trade:

National Book Network, Inc.
4720 Boston Way
Lanham, MD 20706
1-800-462-6420

Library of Congress Catalog Card Number 96-71269
Wolfe, Rebecca Luhn
Politics That Work
ISBN 1-56052-445-6

This book is printed on recyclable paper with soy ink.

10 9 8 7 6 5 4 3 2

LEARNING OBJECTIVES FOR:

OFFICE POLITICS

The objectives for *Office Politics* are listed below. They have been developed to guide you, the reader, to the core issues covered in this book.

Objectives

❏ 1) **To discuss the need for being political in the workplace**

❏ 2) **To explain positive political techniques**

❏ 3) **To explain strategies of political negotiating**

❏ 4) **To discuss negative politics and to show how to deal with them**

Assessing Your Progress

In addition to the Learning Objectives, *Office Politics* includes a unique new **assessment tool*** which can be found at the back of this book. A twenty-five item, multiple choice/true-false questionnaire allows the reader to evaluate his or her comprehension of the subject matter covered. An answer sheet, with a chart matching the questions to the listed objectives, is also provided.

* Assessments should not be used in any selection process.

ABOUT THE AUTHOR

Rebecca Luhn Wolfe, Ph.D., is president of Innovative Consulting Services, a Houston-based training firm. She has been involved in corporate business education for several years, including positions held as director of training for a large health care management firm and for a major airline. Dr. Luhn's interest in business and professional development has resulted in the publication of four other books, *Buying Your First Franchise, Managing Anger, Systematic Succession Planning* and *Employee Benefits with Cost Control* by Crisp Publications, Inc., and academic works on file in many universities. Dr. Luhn earned a Ph.D. in Business Communications and also holds the Distinguished Americans award for her contributions to education. She often lectures at Rice University and the University of Houston.

In addition to writing, her focus is providing consulting services with a range of expertise in business for both small and large corporations.

ABOUT THE SERIES

With over 200 titles in print, the acclaimed Crisp 50-Minute™ series presents self-paced learning at its easiest and best. These comprehensive self-study books for business or personal use are filled with exercises, activities, assessments, and case studies that capture your interest and increase your understanding.

Other Crisp products, based on the 50-Minute™ books, are available in a variety of learning style formats for both individual and group study, including audio, video, CD-ROM, and computer-based training.

Dedication

To Mike Crisp for giving so many the power of knowledge and to Phil Gerould for providing the advantage through opportunity. Thank you Crisp Publications for giving so much to so many.

CONTENTS

CONTENTS (continued)

INTRODUCTION

Businesses of all sizes have changed drastically in the past decade of down-sizing, reorganizing, re-engineering, joint ventures and hostile takeovers. Office politics have also changed, though most executives don't acknowledge it. No longer just a "power game," office politics is now an important skill for developing a competitive edge and surviving in a global marketplace. Practical and ethical political tactics should be taught at every job level. Having political savvy is vital to the success of talented individuals in a fiercely competitive world.

Politics can have positive results if we understand the tactics and strategies that are necessary in the workplace and distinguish between good and bad politicking. *Politics That Work* shows you how to make informed career choices, deal with negative tactics, practice correct strategies, become a good communicator, and master negotiations.

You will also learn how powerful mutual understanding and respect can be in the workplace, how to remain flexible and make concessions without losing, and how to deal with unfair situations with confidence and diplomacy. Life is not always fair, but there are advantages to practicing fair, sensible, and ethical politics.

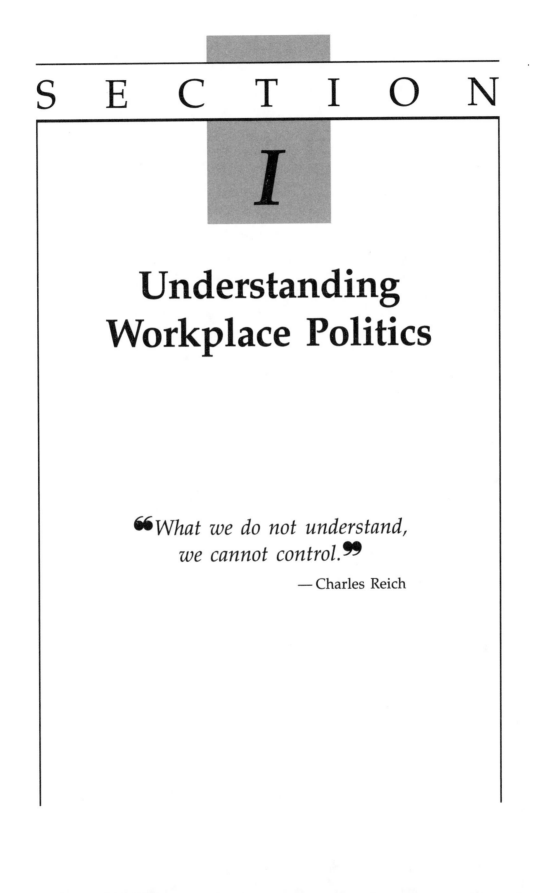

SECTION

I

Understanding
Workplace Politics

*"What we do not understand,
we cannot control."*

— Charles Reich

THE MEANING OF OFFICE POLITICS

Office politics are often not discussed, acknowledged or even recognized. But in recent years reasonable and responsible office politics have been acknowledged as great skills in the business world. It is likewise known that negative, deceptive and unethical practices can lead to disaster in the workplace.

Those who understand the difference between ethical and unethical practices have developed common sense savvy and communication skills that go far beyond what they learned in management classes. Such skills are born of practice and determination.

Are office politics truly a game? That depends on your attitude. If you take your career seriously and are in it for the long haul, then you will find that it can be a series of games with the goal of becoming a champion. If you think that games in business are not healthy, then consider the following:

1. All business is competitive.

2. All teams have a leader.

3. Champions are well-rewarded.

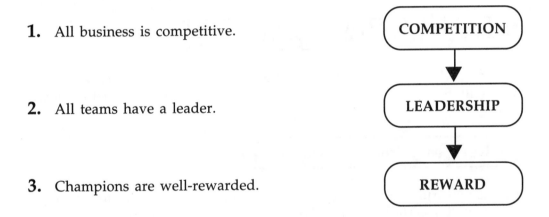

The political arena does not have to turn into a circus or a hunt in which only one person survives. Business requires strategic planning, theory, tactics, and maneuvers. Your career requires these same elements.

Since office politics are the strategies that everyone in both public and private organizations uses to gain or maintain a competitive advantage in their business, you can choose to become politically skilled and position yourself for greater opportunities and success in life.

It can be confusing to deal with people who have very one-sided agendas and use unethical practices. Your goal is to develop ethical practices, as well as to recognize others' "I win, you lose" strategies and overcome them.

THE MEANING OF OFFICE POLITICS
(continued)

As you understand the true meaning of politics—their power—and take action and find solutions, you will soon be capable of dealing with and maintaining personal control over most office situations.

Five Simple Rules

Understand Your Corporate System

Learning the ways of your company's culture can only get you off to a good start. Unless you are in a position to change policy, you should follow it.

Know When to Hold and When to Fold

Knowing when to hold tight to your beliefs and when to concede is a valuable skill. Since neither way is always right or wrong, you must be flexible.

Believe in Win-Win Situations

Unless you truly believe in creating win-win situations, you may never master politics. The art of negotiating can be a great survival tool.

Play Fair

Even when being attacked by others, always show that you are a fair and ethical player. Never play the game on their level; you could go down in the first round.

Think First, Act Later

Never let your emotions dictate action before you have time to think about your desired outcome. If you focus on control at the time, you will produce a better result later.

SELF-CHECK

Place a check by each statement you practice.

❏ I always look and act calm, even if I am outraged.

❏ I show respect to all people at all levels of work.

❏ I never give details about my personal feelings.

❏ I always try to say the right thing.

❏ I believe honesty has its own rewards.

Congratulations if you checked them all. You have a good sense of successful politics.

POLITICS HAS CHANGED

Office politics is now out of the closet in most companies, and it is common knowledge that tactics do not have to be unethical to work. While some people may not know how to be politically fair, many have learned that political fairness works wonders, and are studying the political habits of our most admired business leaders.

These changes are not only good for a competitive edge in business, but they open up a whole new area for learning the value and necessity of advanced communication skills. It gives each employee at all job levels an opportunity to compete and excel on level ground—a far healthier environment than the silenced organizations of the past.

Although with this new political transformation, you will often find a new leadership emerging. There is a renewal of strong values in business today and our new political awareness can help employees focus on purpose rather than problems.

The Good and the Bad

Of course there is good and bad to most everything in business and life. But just because there is bad doesn't mean that it must be avoided at all cost. Understanding and preparation are essential if we are to do our best when negativity occurs.

Let's begin with an overview of both sides of workplace politics.

GOOD EFFECTS	BAD EFFECTS
Strengthen communication	Promote power games
Make business deals work	Make negotiations difficult
Help people find creative solutions	Hamper productivity and creativity
Increase influence	Undermine authority
Create an atmosphere of respect	Create bad feelings
Help people avoid destructive behavior	Encourage vicious smear campaigns
Make employees adaptable to change	Hurt healthy corporate climates
Offer competitive career advantage	Bring out the worst in obsessive people
Build self-confidence	Weaken the naive and already weak
Foster excellence and innovation	Cover up the truth
Strengthen decision-making skills	Encourage lying and deception

As you can see from the list, it can go either way. The difference depends upon your intention. So, if political issues are used for negative reasons and personal power without regard for the company or for others, will the outcome obviously be negative? If our focus is on the positive and we take steps to keep the issues honest, will the outcome be successful? It is not quite that simple. In the real world there is deception and unethical behavior. Your mission should never be to change everyone else, but rather to develop you own professional and ethical political behavior. Since not everyone plays by the same rules, you will also want to know how to be prepared to respond and survive when others are not fair. Redirecting negative behavior and attitudes can often be your best strategy, but knowing the right direction can be tricky.

DO YOU NEED TO PLAY THE GAME TO STAY?

You may have your own answer to this question by now, but just in case you do not, let's sort it out. Staying in an organization that is highly political is not necessarily the issue. Staying on top and even getting ahead in a highly political atmosphere can often seem like an abstract thought for most of us. The principles that govern the workplace are really not much different than the fundamental code of conduct for most of life. Beliefs, strategy, and action control the outcomes we experience, personally and professionally. Let's look at Byron's case.

CASE STUDY: *Taken Out to Lunch*

Byron, an energetic and enthusiastic worker, landed his job just out of graduate school at a high-tech company with over four hundred employees who were bright and hungry for advancement and power.

In his first two weeks on the job he had been taken out to lunch by four different people in the company and been "fed" more gossip and advice than he knew what to do with. Not only did these four people dislike one another, but most of the people in Byron's department were at odds with the boss. He was not only disappointed, but confused by his co-workers behavior. Byron confided this to his brother, who said, "You'll learn to play. It's a cut-throat game." Byron vowed to never play the game. When asked if he had been to lunch with any of them again, Byron answered "Yes, I asked Tom, the marketing manager, for some advice because I felt I could trust him." His brother pointed out that, at that point, he had "joined the game."

Author's Comments

Byron should have asked someone outside the company for advice. He was an easy target for the others and just needs some experience. Staying out of the game would have been best for him at this point.

Byron will learn that gossip and negative statements can be cut short, and his co-workers will soon realize that he will not be their victim if he does not listen. The new person can often be caught off guard by power plays, but the best strategy here is silence and awareness. You can choose your moves and avoid getting wiped out at the start of your career. Not taking the bait in even small-minded gossip is a political strategy. Gossip and false advice can seem to be two of the least harmful of negative tactics, but can often damage even the most seasoned players if the ploy works. Remember, not all gossip and rumors are false. If it affects you, then carefully do your homework before taking any action.

There are many other forms of negative and positive politics. Not participating in the negative is part of the positive approach to any workplace political activity. Your advantage comes with knowing the rules and understanding the best moves for your career.

Principles to Follow

- Understand your job and corporate culture
- Stay focused and have solid goals
- Remain flexible and positive
- Always remain a team player
- Communicate effectively
- Be proactive and not reactive
- Be responsible and productive
- Build solid relationships

Use the following statements to assess your level of political drive. There are no right or wrong answers, only whether you agree or disagree. Be honest with yourself.

EXERCISE: *Your Political IQ*

		AGREE	DISAGREE
1.	Without exception, honesty is the best policy.	❏	❏
2.	Never tell anyone something that can be used against you.	❏	❏
3.	Hire only people who will help you get ahead.	❏	❏
4.	Never help out anyone if it doesn't benefit your job.	❏	❏
5.	Take swift action on critical issues.	❏	❏
6.	Power is more important to you than recognition.	❏	❏
7.	Never communicate good ideas if they won't benefit your career.	❏	❏
8.	Your goal is to be the boss of the largest department in your company	❏	❏
9.	If someone shares confidential information, you will disclose it if it is to your advantage.	❏	❏
10.	A good job performance outweighs diplomacy.	❏	❏
11.	It's okay to publicly complain about your employer if you have a gripe.	❏	❏
12.	It's okay to betray a friend if it benefits your career.	❏	❏
13.	It's okay to use someone else's idea and take the credit.	❏	❏

	AGREE	DISAGREE
14. Its advantageous to tell everyone when you've worked on a successful project.	❏	❏
15. It's good to keep a secret if it helped a friend get ahead.	❏	❏
16. When you become angry at a co-worker, you let everyone know why.	❏	❏
17. It is sometimes appropriate to make others feel bad about their work.	❏	❏
18. Never discuss current issues without knowing where others stand first.	❏	❏
19. Never hire anyone who you think is smarter than you.	❏	❏
20. Tell top executives what you think they want to hear.	❏	❏
21. Most people are truthful and honest.	❏	❏
22. Getting revenge is harmful, but getting even can help you.	❏	❏
23. It's okay to tell someone you like their work even if you don't.	❏	❏
24. Intimidation works when all else fails.	❏	❏
25. Staying on a team is okay, but being the leader is what really counts.	❏	❏

CHECK YOUR SCORE

Give yourself the following points for your answers:

No.	Agree	Disagree	No.	Agree	Disagree
1.	1	3	14.	3	0
2.	3	0	15.	3	1
3.	3	1	16.	3	1
4.	3	1	17.	3	1
5.	3	1	18.	3	1
6.	3	1	19.	3	1
7.	3	1	20.	3	0
8.	3	0	21.	1	3
9.	3	1	22.	1	3
10.	1	3	23.	3	0
11.	0	3	24.	3	1
12.	3	1	25.	3	0
13.	3	1			

Interpret Your Score

Range

55–75   You are obsessed with power to a point that it is unhealthy for yourself and those around you. This is beyond the norms and there is very little behavior you wouldn't consider for political gain.

30–54   You crave and love power. Some may consider you ruthless and it can appear that politicking is your career. While your politics may bring you great success, your lust for power may be at the expense of your ethics.

20–29   You are an average politician with skill and diplomacy. Your ethics are strong, but so is your drive. You are wise and controlled with your actions.

Below 20   You may try to practice office politics, but you just don't bother enough to make it a skill. If an opportunity lands at your feet, you may take advantage of it, but not often enough for it to make a difference in your career.

S E C T I O N

II

The Way It Is

> **“**Most powerful is he who has himself in his own power.**”**
>
> —Seneca

WHY POLITICAL SITUATIONS ARE COMMON

To say that politicking occurs everyday in business is an understatement. It is far more common than most even admit. Most political activity is petty, a waste of time, and not necessarily supportive of good business goals.

Everyday Political Practices

Some of the following everyday practices may be familiar to you:

- Being openly criticized in a meeting

- Having a job promotion given to someone with less experience

- Being the scapegoat for someone else's mistake

- Having a project canceled when you are close to finishing it

- Passing on a rumor

- Throwing a large birthday party for a top executive

WHY POLITICAL SITUATIONS
ARE COMMON (continued)

List some of the everyday political practices you are familiar with. What were their outcomes?

► **Situation**: _____

_____

_____

Outcome: _____

_____

► **Situation**: _____

_____

_____

Outcome: _____

_____

► **Situation**: _____

_____

_____

Outcome: _____

_____

Let's review a case study that could have had a happier ending with one small political skill.

> ## CASE STUDY: Jack's Lack of Social Skills
>
> Jack's job as marketing manager was a satisfying career choice for him. He had been in the position for seven years and was highly respected. So when Jack's boss retired and Jack was not offered the position, he was highly disappointed. Jack asked his boss and friend for the past seven years why he did not get the job. His boss stated that there was no one reason, but that some people at the top felt Bob was the better choice because they knew him better. His final advice to Jack was to be a bit more social and to get more exposure in the company.

Author's Comments

Jack did not get the job because he had never politicked for it. It is a competitive world regarding not only skill and experience, but also exposure. Jack had the ability and experience to head the department, but he had not positioned himself for exposure beyond his own boss. Sometimes the person in the front row will be called on first.

Jack's case is an excellent example of how politics could have had a positive result. Unfortunately for Jack, the positive outcome was for Bob. There are many strategies that can be used to gain a competitive advantage.

Long-Term Political Strategies

- Socializing in the organization
- Networking
- Maintaining control and focus
- Setting goals
- Displaying an excellent attitude
- Learning to negotiate
- Communicating persuasively
- Remaining patient

These long-term strategies are a foundation upon which master politicians are able to improve constantly and perform consistently at levels beyond the norm.

WHY POLITICAL SITUATIONS
ARE COMMON (continued)

Your Personal Situation

Take a few minutes to think about what has happened to you in regard to workplace politics and answer the following questions:

► When you recognize a political circumstance that involves you, what usually happens?

_____

_____

► If office conditions force you to accept a negative career outcome, what happens the next time you prepare yourself for a career move?

_____

_____

► What long-term political strategies have you developed for yourself?

_____

_____

► What are your strengths and weaknesses in workplace politics?

_____

_____

► What political skills do you admire in others and would like to acquire for yourself?

_____

_____

► What is your overall attitude about using tactics and strategy to improve your position and political savvy in the workplace?

_____

_____

► What do you feel will be your greatest political challenge in your current company?

_____

_____

YOUR TRUE CHOICES

There are some who believe that politicking is nothing more than a circus. Others accept the practice with open arms, do not regard it as a game, and believe that being politically skilled and educated plays as much a part of advancing in their careers as leadership skills.

The truth is that it is difficult to move forward in your career without engaging in some form of political activity. Most who go out of their way to avoid office politics will find themselves frustrated, angry, and out of the limelight. It may not sound like it, but you do have choices. Consider some levels on which to engage in positive politicking.

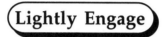

Lightly Engage

You can engage in some activities without considering yourself "a political person." The following behaviors can only benefit you as a person and provide you with a positive approach to your career development:

- Building relationships

- Networking

- Team involvement

- Persuasive communications

Moderately Engage

To go beyond the basics of career development, you would include the following:

- Negotiation tactics

- Making yourself known and visible

- Self-promotion

- Seeking additional responsibility

- Gathering information

- Maintaining emotional self-control

- Projecting a successful image

- Knowing your competition

- Cultivating organizational resources

- Obtaining access to top executives

- Developing advanced communication skills

- Working on important projects

- Complimenting and supporting decision makers

- Maintaining confidence

- Developing followers

Heavily Engage

Those at the highest level of political engagement who crave power and who work toward maintaining control, will also use the following strategies, all of which are considered legitimate and ethical:

- Cultivating relationships outside the company

- Socializing only with the most influential people

- Doing everything to impress higher-ranking people

- Modeling themselves after the best in the business

- Always controlling their behavior

- Becoming experts in their field

- Making things happen

- Leaving nothing to chance

When political actions move into lies and deception, we are no longer dealing with people who have an honest sense of morality and ethics. These tactics, as well as advice for dealing with them, will be discussed later.

MAKING CHANGES

As you review your choices, start to consider the areas in which you would like to change. If you have an emotional resistance to politicking, select ones that will provide you with an opportunity for personal growth. You may think, "That just isn't me," but since all change encounters some form of resistance, you'll never know until you try. Achieving greater personal and professional power involves taking risks. Many strategies will create a degree of discomfort at first, but as with any newly learned skill, you will relax and grow with practice.

Consider a political challenge you have encountered in the past. Identify what happened, how it affected you, and what strategies you could use that would help if this type of situation occurred again.

▶ Political challenge: _____

_____

▶ Result: _____

_____

▶ Strategic solution: _____

_____

As you identify political activities within your organization, consider how your *perceptions of events* determine your *response:*

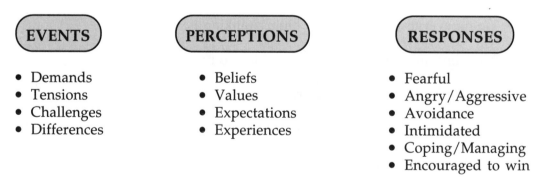

EVENTS	PERCEPTIONS	RESPONSES
• Demands	• Beliefs	• Fearful
• Tensions	• Values	• Angry/Aggressive
• Challenges	• Expectations	• Avoidance
• Differences	• Experiences	• Intimidated
		• Coping/Managing
		• Encouraged to win

As you can see, you do have choices when it comes to participating in, controlling, or coping with workplace politics. The choices are not always clear, but as with most things in life, it is your decisions, not the conditions, that will create your future. You may not always be able to control the situation, but you can control your actions.

THE ENDLESS CAMPAIGN

As with any progressive action, your political campaign must contain key elements and remain flexible throughout your career. The building blocks of a political campaign are mission statement, performance objectives, empowerment commitments, strategies and tactics, communication exchanges, and effectiveness reviews.

Campaign Building Blocks

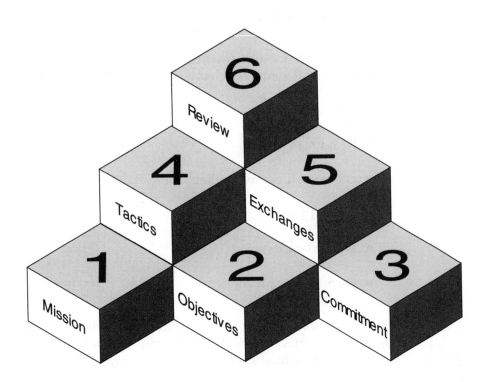

Mission Statement—what you personally and professionally aspire to with regard to workplace politics. For example: To become more politically advanced with proven strategies in order to gain power and visibility and enhance my career.

THE ENDLESS CAMPAIGN (continued)

Your Performance Objectives—the goals or desired outcomes of your campaign. For example:

- To be more skilled in political activity

- To advance in my company

- To gain power and control in my career

- To handle political situations of any nature with ease and confidence

Empowerment Commitments—the attitudes you assume in order to master personal change and growth. For example:

- Develop a positive approach

- Remain flexible

- Let go of negative beliefs

- Learn to focus

- Make decisions

- Become a team player

Strategies and Tactics—the specific methods (strategies) and skills (tactics) you will use to gain the political knowledge and advantage needed to move forward. For example:

- Learn negotiation skills

- Improve your image

- Socialize more

- Develop a network

- Control your responses and reaction

Communication Exchanges—how you network, cultivate information sources, and build relationships. For example:

- Get to know as many people as possible inside and outside the company.

- Keep a file of important facts on key people.

- Engage in new social activities.

- Gather valuable information about your company and the competition.

- Volunteer for activities in the company and your community.

- Keep your name in front of key people.

- Do favors and ask for help when you need it.

Effectiveness Review—monitoring your advancement and progress. For example:

> Set up a chart of activities you have engaged in and record events and their outcome.

As you can see from these campaign building blocks, this can be an extensive and long-term project. Once you become more skilled in your own political activity and learn to recognize the tactics of others, the process will not be as involved or detailed. Our examples are very general, so when setting up your own plan, be specific to your career and related business activities.

Now take a few minutes to get ahead. Start on your campaign by filling in the following worksheet.

POLITICAL CAMPAIGN WORKSHEET

► Personal and Professional Political Mission:

_____

_____

► Political Performance Objectives:

1. _____

2. _____

3. _____

► Political Empowerment Commitment:

1. _____

2. _____

3. _____

► Political Strategies and Tactics:

1. _____

2. _____

3. _____

► Communication Exchanges:

1. _____

2. _____

3. _____

► Effectiveness Review:

1. _____

2. _____

3. _____

HOW POWER ENABLES

The word "power" means many things to many people. It also can be applied to hundreds of different areas in business and life. But for the purpose of this book, we will consider "power" to be *the ability to get things done, obtain results, influence others, and project control.*

Power is both desirable and misunderstood. Power can be abusive, but for now our focus will be on the very positive effects and rewards of power. Where does power come from?

People sometimes believe that power comes with a title, that you can buy it, or that you simply have to earn it. All of these can be true to some extent, but most power comes from within yourself and involves learning—from knowledge, understanding, and experience. These give us access to opportunity and advancement in our personal and professional life. Power enables you to:

- influence others
- direct your future
- achieve goals
- experience fulfillment
- establish resources
- control emotions
- expand on innovation

- welcome change and make changes
- exercise authority
- help others out
- be competitive with an advantage
- maximize performance
- open up opportunities

List some goals that power would enable you to accomplish:

Your Power Vision

1. _____

2. _____

3. _____

4. _____

5. _____

HOW POWER ENABLES (continued)

CASE STUDY: Power from Within

After working for years as a service representative, Sherry had just obtained a new and rather large account for the company and been promoted to account executive. The annual sales conference was her first opportunity to give a professional presentation. The fear was overwhelming, but she did not dare back out or let her fear render her powerless. She took matters into her own hands and began her campaign. First, she asked for help from two of the best and most admired speakers in the company and signed up for evening classes on presentation skills. She got help with her slide presentation from a designer in the graphics department in return for crediting him at the conference and letting his boss know how valuable he is to the sales division. Her slides were spectacular, her presentation was professional and her boss was quite pleased.

Author's Response

What Sherry did was to turn a possibly crippling situation into a personal achievement. She created power for herself by positioning herself to succeed. First, she used available resources for her help. Second, she overcame her fear with knowledge, and learned presentation skills. Third, she negotiated and gave credit where it was due.

Not all stories have such a happy ending, but there are solutions to even the most difficult situations. What may be easy for one person can be crippling to another. To help ourselves, we must often turn to others for assistance. As for Sherry, well, she is on the right track. She will be remembered by her boss, her peers, the people who helped her, and by the graphics department for the credit she gave them. But most of all, Sherry will remember the experience, use it for a future advantage, and one day she will in turn help someone else. Sherry is establishing power.

MASTERS OF THE GAME
(HOW THEY WORK)

The best political strategists know how to get things done, and to do it to their advantage, by:

- Being driven (and driving others) to succeed

- Taking risks that generate rewards

- Producing growth

- Creating positive results

- Controlling their destiny

- Surviving and recovering from mistakes

- Competing and winning

- Knowing the best influential techniques

- Setting and changing the rules to their advantage

- Knowing the best-kept secrets

The best know how to unleash their power. They not only take advantage of opportunity, but they often create it. The masters we are referring to do not cross over the line to deception or devious tactics. They may be driven, but their power plays are not unethical. They draw power from those below and above them. Their agendas are strong and their tasks are rarely easy.

Do you have what it takes to become a political master?

S E C T I O N

III

Politics Can Improve Your Career

"*What happens is not as important as how you react to what happens.***"**

—Thaddeus Golas

HOW TO REMAIN POLITICALLY CORRECT

It can be difficult for even the most skilled politician to act "correctly" in difficult situations that cause not only disruption, but blunders that are quite hard to recover from. For example:

- Supporting your boss when you know he or she is wrong.

- Being made the scapegoat for your boss' mistakes.

- Having someone come to you with negative gossip.

- Having someone at the "top" ask you to do something you do not agree with.

- Being asked to correct a co-worker's mistake.

- Having a friend and co-worker ask you to share confidential information you have access to.

- Saying the wrong thing in a really important meeting.

- Having someone else take credit for your idea.

- Knowing something that could harm a project or your company.

- Being asked to support promotions for people when you know they cannot do the job.

These and many other political situations are difficult because they can affect you and others negatively, or go against beliefs you have. They are political in that there is a decision on whether and how to act that could be an advantage or a disadvantage for yourself and/or others.

Not all difficult situations are political and not all political situations are difficult. We face many difficulties in business that have nothing to do with a political motive.

If something occurs that is illegal or dishonest, even if the action was politically motivated, then we must say that there is a right or wrong answer to the problem. But in most difficult situations there are no concrete answers.

How to Make the Best Decision

The "best" decision is one in which everyone wins. If that is not possible, then there are some considerations in deciding whether or not to act.

THE POWER OF FOCUS

The "power of focus" in any decision entails looking at the big picture. Often just the slightest adjustment to the scope of your focus can bring a much clearer understanding to the situation. It is always better to step back and assess the problem before responding. In addition to buying additional time, you focus on a solution to the problem at hand rather than jumping to a faulty decision. Although business often requires rapid decisions, making the right decision under pressure can be difficult without practice and without using some proven techniques. The following questions are known to help leaders in making better decisions:

1. Are you hearing about what is the real issue or even the facts in a situation? (Do you need to investigate?)

2. How and where did the problem or situation originate, and is the problem more involved than is being stated?

3. Does the situation require any action, and what could the end result be?

4. How does this problem truly affect you, and how would it affect you if you take a particular position on it?

5. How do you truly feel about the situation, and are your feelings or thinking accurate?

Your conclusion should come down to the following:

- What do you want to do about this situation, if anything?

- Who will be affected by this decision or action?

- What is your final strategy going to be?

Review the following case study and answer the questions to assess the situation and come up with the best solution.

CASE STUDY: *The Breakfast Club*

Marshall was the new member at the Executive Communications Breakfast Club, a group of some of the most successful executives in the field of cellular communications. Marshall just listened for a few months but, feeling compelled to impress his peers, he began to contribute his own tales of "big deals," insider information, and good-old-fashioned gossip.

Unfortunately, he got a little carried away with what he claimed to be "very confidential information." He told the man sitting next to him that his next-door neighbor, Janice, worked for On-The-Line Cellular Corp., and had said there was going to be a huge divisional shake up. He went on to say that the new V.P. of Accounts was going to bring in his own people, and that this man was controlling and power hungry.

Well, it turned out that Marshall was talking to that new V.P. at On-The-Line, who just happened to forget his name tag that morning.

What Do You Think?

▶ Who had the real problem here; Marshall, the V.P., or Janice? Why?

_____

_____

▶ Who made the first political blunder?

_____

_____

▶ Who had the most to lose by this gossip?

_____

_____

HOW TO REMAIN POLITICALLY CORRECT (continued)

► What should be done about the situation, if anything?

_____

_____

► Should Marshall skip the breakfast from now on?

_____

_____

► Do you think Janice's job is now on the line?

_____

_____

► Is recovery possible for Janice or Marshall? If so, how? If not, why not?

_____

_____

RECOGNIZING AND RECOVERING FROM MISTAKES

Other than that which is obvious, like Marshall's mistake, how can you tell if you have made a political blunder. Not all political mistakes are so easily discovered. They may not manifest for days, weeks, or months. They can show up just when you least expect it and often you do not remember the event.

An example might be in a job evaluation, when your boss points out your poor communication skills and says how you offended a top client in a meeting months earlier. It may never be directly pointed out, but these blunders can come back to haunt you if you do not learn to recognize your own mistakes.

Many people make politically incorrect statements in meetings or group sessions. Let's say you do or say something wrong in a meeting, or at least are perceived that way by others. If, indeed, you do not see it as they do, meant no harm, or perhaps were just joking, you may never realize that you blundered. The sooner you recognize you own mistakes, the sooner you can recover from them. You know you have said the wrong thing if:

- The room becomes very quiet and all eyes are on you.

- Your co-worker leans over to you and says, "What were you thinking?"

- Your leader suggests a sudden break.

- Someone suggests that the subject be changed.

- Your boss is there and asks to see you after the meeting.

- Everyone laughs and you did not mean to be funny.

- You are asked to explain yourself—now!

- Everyone pretends to start taking notes.

- You are skipped over for any suggestions in that meeting.

RECOGNIZING AND RECOVERING FROM MISTAKES (continued)

What are some alternatives for recovery?

- You can admit that you just made a mistake with what you said and apologize.

- You can try to correct yourself with a new statement.

- You can excuse yourself from the meeting.

- Put a smile on your face, remain calm, and move past the statement.

There is truly no easy out when you have fallen into this circumstance. If recovery is not possible at the time, you can always apologize to key people at a later time, but do not wait too long. The more time people have to talk about what you did, the bigger the event becomes. Once you apologize, forget it and *do not* discuss the event with co-workers or peers. If your boss wants to talk about it, then he or she should be the only one you go over it with. The less you fuel the fire, the faster it will go out.

We have all blundered in one way or another. It is embarrassing, to say the least, but move on and do not belabor the issue. Someone else will come along with a new problem and the focus will be off of you. Keep this in mind when you gossip about someone else's mistake. It could happen to you tomorrow.

HOW TO USE POLITICAL CORRECTNESS

Using politics to your advantage in difficult situations, or just using it at all can be tricky. It can also be quite advantageous. Just as political blunders can have a profound effect, so can intentionally being politically correct.

> ## CASE STUDY: *Politically Correct Recovery*
>
> When Judy became the public relations director for Grand Destination Airlines, she was new to the city and the airline, but not the type of work.
>
> At a PR bash for a new nonstop route the airline would be flying, she mistakenly overlooked seating Peggy Stanton, the special events reporter for a local station with the other important people at the head table. After three years of getting very little cooperation or reporting from Peggy, Judy learned from another of the station's reporters just how offended Peggy was about the earlier event.
>
> At the next event, Judy not only placed Peggy at the head table, but acknowledged her social stupidity to Peggy, apologized for the error and explained that she had meant no harm.
>
> Peggy pretended to never have been offended, but you can believe that things were flying much higher for the airline and their PR director from that day forward with the help of a new friend and influential reporter.

Author's Comments

As you can see, Judy not only took advantage of the touchy political situation, she made an incredible recovery from a blunder she made years earlier. Judy used politics to her advantage. It took her some time to discover her error, but as you can see, recovery is always possible. Of course, it would have saved Judy a few years of anguish if she had investigated the problem earlier.

HOW TO USE POLITICAL CORRECTNESS
(continued)

> ## CASE STUDY: *Political Advantage*
>
> Called back for his final interview with the CEO of a company he had longed to work for, Jason had done his homework on the company and brushed up on his interviewing skills, but could not quite figure out the edge he would need over the other equally talented applicants.
>
> Jason called the company's Human Resource department and skillfully discovered that it was the CEO who determined who got the job in almost all departments.
>
> While Jason waited outside the main office, he flipped through several magazines—including *Men's Fitness* and *Running Magazine*—all addressed to the CEO.
>
> You can just guess what happened when the CEO asked Jason about his hobbies. Though Jason did work out at the health club but only rarely jogged, he capitalized on his experiences to establish a special connection with the CEO. Jason got the job and took up jogging four days a week.

It was a *small* political move that Jason made, but it gave him the advantage and it worked. Advantage is usually the motivation that drives political activity.

Use politics to your advantage without stooping to abuse.

Keys to Positive Politicking

- Visualize positive outcomes
- Focus on the facts
- Control impulses
- Look for solutions
- Understand motives
- Recognize what you want
- Use value judgment

WHAT IT MEANS TO BE POLITICALLY CORRECT

Many people think that being politically correct means doing only what is accepted by the majority. That is somewhat simplistic for the business environment.

Situations can become so involved that it may be impossible to know the majority position. Many people in top business positions are on what is called "a need to know basis." While many executives refuse to put their reputation and careers on the line without details, they often do not receive the full explanations that they long for, or they may hear a rather altered version of the truth. These circumstances can create tension, conflict, and confusion within an organization. To be objective under such conditions, you should remain politically wise.

Politically Wise Decision Making

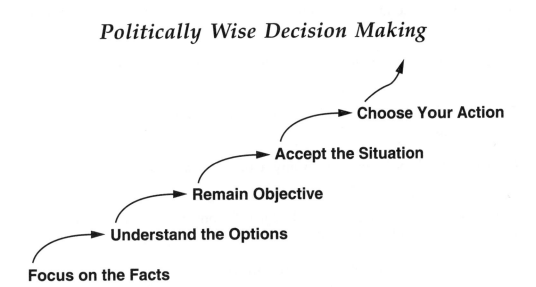

Some things are out of your control and most high-level politically driven decisions are never made entirely clear to all involved. It is often the reactions and frustration of these experiences that lead people to act counter-productively in the face of incomplete information.

If you have a hard time remaining politically correct in difficult situations or under circumstances you can't control, you may have to alter your thinking to survive in a business world filled with uncertainty.

WHAT IT MEANS TO BE POLITICALLY CORRECT (continued)

How to Work with Uncertainty

1. Identify your negative thoughts about political activity in the workplace.

2. Review the evidence and never assume that what you hear or see is fact.

3. Think in terms of multiple possibilities instead of viewing situations one-sidedly.

4. Before you announce your assessment of a situation, ask a few trusted people their thoughts on your views.

5. Search out the meaning behind a situation before you decide what is acceptable.

6. Define what you will accept before you pass judgment or make any decision.

7. Do not assume you know all the facts or all the reasons why something has occurred.

8. Do a cost–benefit analysis of any action you may take.

In your efforts to remain politically correct, you will soon discover the following benefits to not compromising values and ethics:

- Gaining the trust of those with influence

- Accessing more information

- Obtaining more authority

- Developing more contacts

- Protecting your position

- Being involved in decision making

List some benefits you could derive from developing politically correct skills in your company.

▶ **Political Skill:** _____

_____

_____

Possible Benefit: _____

_____

_____

▶ **Political Skill:** _____

_____

_____

Possible Benefit: _____

_____

_____

SECTION

IV

Devious Tactics
Can Destroy

66We are never so easily deceived as when
we imagine we are deceiving others.99

—La Rochefoucauld

RECOGNIZE DEVIOUS TACTICS

Although our goal has been to stress the positive side to workplace politics, the fact is that there is far too much devious activity in business.

A tactic can be devious without being illegal. It is safe to say that illegal activity is, without a doubt, the wrong way to conduct yourself. But other devious, deceitful, malicious, and false behavior can be a question of your own values or beliefs. Some people believe that all is fair; but, for most, unethical tactics are *wrong!*

When a situation violates human rights or involves dishonesty, cruelty, abuse, cheating, or hostility; you are dealing with people who are power hungry, who will destroy anything that gets in their way, and who take huge risks with their careers. Fortunately, these people usually self-destruct, but they can do a great deal of damage before going down.

While not illegal, many tactics are, by all means, unfair and devious. Review these tactics and ways to protect yourself from them.

Tactic: False Support

If someone gives you false encouragement, you will often move forward with what is really bad advice.

EXAMPLE: *Although your boss is too proud of his new marketing plan to take criticism, and will black-list any employee that provides it, someone tells you that the boss would love to see a suggestion list of all the things wrong with his plan.*

ADVICE: Always think about a suggestion that could affect your career. You must investigate and never act simply on someone else's advice.

48

RECOGNIZE DEVIOUS TACTICS (continued)

Tactic: Discrediting

Damaging statements are frequently used to discredit others. They can be negative statements about you, questions concerning your ability to work on a project, or false concerns about you.

EXAMPLE: *A co-worker says to your boss that he will give you a call later because you seemed tense and have complained of a hangover every day this week.*

ADVICE: There is not much you can do to stop someone from lying about you, but you can address the statement if you hear about it afterward.

Tactic: Back Stabbing

The back-stabber is never very original and sometimes all too obvious. Someone befriends you, seems to be very nice, but has in mind to ruin your image or career.

EXAMPLE: *A co-worker provokes you into a conversation about how you really feel about the new boss. You express yourself and make some negative comments. The back-stabber then goes to the boss saying how happy he or she is to be working with her, but hopes that you will come around and feel better about things.*

ADVICE: Do not question all of your new friendships, but always play it safe. If you never say anything bad or negative, others will have nothing to repeat unless they make it up.

Tactic: Stealing Ideas

People who are insecure and cannot work in teams may take credit for something they did not do. They generally hear or see an idea that they know will receive recognition and then pass it off as their own.

EXAMPLE: *In working on an idea to save your department a great deal of money, you share your proposal with a co-worker, who, while offering you advice on fine tuning it, turns in the proposal as his own.*

ADVICE: Well, a thief is a thief, but it is harder to steal what is protected. If you do have a good idea, put the basic concept in writing and distribute it with a note that the final proposal will be out soon. Let others know. If your idea is stolen from a group session, then others will know it was yours, but in one-on-one meetings, do not leave yourself open for theft.

Tactic: Crippling

This devious political act is designed to injure you just enough that you will take your own fatal fall. The crippler constantly undermines and destroys your self-confidence with put-downs, negative comments, and statements that lead you to believe others do not like you. You feel worthless to the point of being unproductive.

EXAMPLE: *The boss sends back your work with a note that says "Unacceptable" or dismisses your ideas, calls you stupid, or suggests you never do anything right.*

ADVICE: It is difficult to take such abuse, but you must hold out, believe in yourself, and position yourself to move forward in your career without being destroyed. Stay positive, and consider finding a new job or position if you find your attitude and self-esteem being undermined.

RECOGNIZE DEVIOUS TACTICS (continued)

Tactic: Emotional Blackmail

Those who practice blackmail are one of the most serious kinds of deviants. To gain advantage and power, they will threaten to disclose something you have done that will make you look bad or could ruin your career if it were brought out in the open.

EXAMPLE: *An emotional blackmailer discovers that you have taken kickbacks from one of your vendors. She demands a pay raise and threatens to expose your activity if her demands are not met.*

ADVICE: Extortion has never been easy to deal with and you do not have to be doing anything wrong in your current job to have someone dig up something from your past that you do not want exposed. Stay clear in your activities and come clean with your past if exposed.

Tactic: Zoning

This method of divide and conquer is attempted by many managers. The tactic is to create dissension among the departments in order to gain power and control.

EXAMPLE: *The district manager hints to the Sales Department that Service has been holding them back and creating bad feelings with clients. He then turns around and tells Service that Sales is making false promises that lead to unrealistic expectations for the Service Department.*

ADVICE: Question what you hear and open up lines of communication with other departments. Meet with those you have working relationships with and discuss problem areas.

Tactic: Unacceptable Conditions

Making conditions so miserable for employees who can't be fired because of excellent work performance, is a strategy used by bosses who want someone out of the company.

EXAMPLE: *Your boss assigns you to projects that are meaningless, or makes you travel twenty days out of thirty, knowing that you dislike being on the road. Also, you are excluded from activities that other co-workers engage in weekly, such as staff meetings.*

ADVICE: Often people who have authority over you are hard to cope with. Your strategy is to position yourself for another job in the company. Chances are that conditions will not change as long as that person is determined to get rid of you. If you do not know why this is happening you could try to open up communications and confront the person directly.

Think back on tactics you have encountered, their result, how you responded, and the disarming technique you could have (should have) used—the way you will handle it next time.

	TACTIC USED	RESULT & RESPONSE	DISARMING TECHNIQUE
1.			
2.			
3.			

AVOID THE ATTACKERS

We have given you some strategies for dealing with people who play devious political games. Confronting and exposing are two options, but what do you do about that one person who has zeroed in on you with destruction in mind?

First of all, hold your position. You can become unproductive and exhausted trying to outmaneuver this attacker. Your best strategy is to maintain control over yourself and your territory.

► *Establish Allies*

Your defense is always stronger if you are a welcomed member of a team and a valued peer.

► *Analyze the Conflict*

Discover the real issues behind the attacks and the person's motivation.

► *Find Your Vulnerable Spots*

Realize any areas of vulnerability that you may have and work to close them off.

► *Understand Your Options*

Find out what legal recourse you have, if any, and what your options are for dealing with the attacks.

► *Create Distance*

Never run, but if you create distance, you can give the attacker a chance to get confused about direction.

► *Remain Confident*

The attacker enjoys seeing fear in the victim.

► *Stick to Your Agenda*

The attacker's intent is to throw you off balance so that you are an easier target. Stick to your professional and personal goals, but it is not necessary to announce your itinerary.

NEVER LOSE CONTROL

Whatever you do in a difficult or impossible situation, remain in control of your emotions. You have every right to be angry and even outraged at betrayal, a vicious smear campaign or any other deceptive political tactic. Losing control and striking back will not improve your situation. Remember attackers are out of control in the first place, and you don't need to contribute to the negative behavior or play by their rules by succumbing to pressure:

- Control your emotions and think rationally.

- Express yourself constructively and ethically.

- Evaluate your feelings and your needs.

- Play only by your rules or the rules of the company.

- Formulate a strategy for dealing with the problem.

Think First, Act Later

Even if you do not lose control, you can make a bad situation worse by taking action too soon or even at all. As we discussed earlier, some political tactics do not require a response, and those that justify a response do not necessarily require an immediate one. Take time to develop a better perspective on the situation. Generally, volatile emotions lead to volatile responses and unproductive results.

NEVER LOSE CONTROL (continued)

> ## CASE STUDY: Mike's Response
>
> Mike was in the middle of a new product proposal when John, a co-worker, interrupted and announced that no one in the department agreed with Mike's ideas or felt this new product was worth the time and money it would take to develop it.
>
> Mike let John finish and then smiled, thanking John for his comments. Mike continued his presentation and the next day had each of his team members sign the proposal showing support for it. He then sent a copy to his boss and the new product development director. It held everyone's signature but John's. Mike had asked him to sign it first and he had refused.

Author's Comments

Although Mike had been outraged by John's ploy, he did nothing in the meeting or say anything to John after the meeting. Mike carefully considered all of his options and knew he had the support of his team members, but not that of John. John never counted on Mike keeping his composure in the meeting; nor did he ever consider the fact that Mike would take a vote of those in favor of his proposal. Mike did play the game of politics when he had to, but he did it with savvy and on his own terms.

Make Your Position Known

Recall a political situation you have been involved in and then answer the following questions:

Political Situation: _____

_____

_____

1. What was your first reaction? _____

    _____

2. Do you feel you were in control? If yes, how? If not, why not?

    _____

    _____

3. How did you communicate your political position? _____

    _____

4. What would you do differently the next time? _____

    _____

5. What have you learned from the experience? _____

    _____

ARE YOU TOO PREDICTABLE?

You can make yourself vulnerable to a devious politician if your responses and actions are predictable. Use the following checklist to assess whether you have behaviors that make you an easy target:

	SOMETIMES	OFTEN
1. I gossip.	❏	❏
2. I get angry.	❏	❏
3. I say what I feel.	❏	❏
4. I am defensive when criticized.	❏	❏
5. I make excuses for mistakes.	❏	❏
6. I know how to pressure others.	❏	❏
7. I exaggerate issues.	❏	❏
8. I'm always agreeable.	❏	❏
9. I can't make a decision.	❏	❏
10. I try to be everyone's friend.	❏	❏
11. I talk behind people's backs.	❏	❏
12. I walk out when upset.	❏	❏
13. I put down others.	❏	❏
14. I try to make others feel guilty.	❏	❏
15. I cover up for others.	❏	❏
16. I tell everything.	❏	❏

Before you try to assess why you end up in political conflicts, assess how your predictability makes you an easy target.

UNDERSTANDING BEHAVIOR

You do not have to be a psychologist to become skilled at protecting yourself from devious politics, but it does help to understand the drive and motivation behind such behavior.

The driving force behind workplace politics is the desire for power, advantage, and control. Politics and winning are an obsession for unethical individuals who, it is safe to say, have very distorted values. Their behavior may be triggered by:

- Hunger for acceptance

- Strong insecurity

- Paranoia

- Obsessive personality

- Basic unhappiness

- Narcissistic personality

- Controlling personality

- Distorted beliefs

- Uncontrollable drive to succeed

Remember, there are no excuses for malicious behavior, but there usually are reasons for it. Knowing what makes people behave this way can help you defuse the potentially deadly tactics of the unethical and ruthless politician.

S E C T I O N

V

The Long and Short of Office Relationships

❝Knowledge of human nature is the beginning and end of political education.❞

—Henry Adams

SUPPORT AT EVERY LEVEL

Even if you are not inclined to engage in serious politicking, it is wise to learn the skills that can cultivate support at every level in your organization. One of the most effective ways to do this is by beginning with "higher-ups." Unless you are the CEO or working directly for one, then chances are there are other people in positions of power over you in your company.

Making friends at the top can help boost an ordinary career to an exceptional career, with the help of lots of hard work, of course. Those at the top can move you forward faster, as well as strengthen your relationships at all levels.

HIGHER-UPS

YOUR BOSS

CLIENTS

SUPPORT AT ALL LEVELS

CO-WORKERS

YOURSELF

SUBORDINATES

Impressing Higher-Ups

- Identify with the best
- Initiate communications
- Be positive and pro-company

- Show respect
- Get on committees
- Volunteer for projects

SUPPORT AT EVERY LEVEL (continued)

Impressing Your Boss

- Learn you boss' goals
- Understand you boss' style
- Help your boss look good

- Do not upstage your boss
- Give your boss advice tactfully
- Support your boss' ideas

Gaining Support from Clients

- Show respect and appreciation
- Be attentive and responsive
- Get to know them and their businesses

- Be diplomatic and professional
- Be available
- Meet deadlines

Gaining Support from Co-Workers

- Be a team player
- Share accomplishments
- Be helpful and sincere

- Be diplomatic and share "wins"
- Ask for help
- Compliment their work

Supporting Yourself

- Invest in yourself
- Display excellent business etiquette
- Always be professional

- Show responsibility
- Accept advice and criticism
- Create solutions, not problems

Gaining Support from Subordinates

- Support their ideas and suggestions
- Give recognition for work well done
- Act promptly on their problems
- Be friendly and helpful
- Be flexible with their requests
- Be respectful to their suggestions

The Need for Support

To become powerful and influential in any organization, it is very important to be respected and valued by those at all levels of the workplace. Cultivating these relationships can only help your career if handled properly. There is no advantage to being a loner in the company. People do exceptional things for people they like. Faking it does not work in the long run. People are very smart and aware of phony friendships. Although your motivation may be for your own personal gain, your attitude and care for others must be genuine. If you bully your way to the top, you can become a very lonely person. The same holds true if you go to extremes to protect yourself from others. Anything you do that makes you feel too different, separated, or disconnected with the majority means you are without support.

CASE STUDY: Unpopular Patty

Patty was let go when her company merged with another. Although her work was well-respected, she was not thought of as a valued team player because she hadn't cultivated any true relationships in the organization. She lacked support from all areas of the company.

When she found a new, though lower, position with less pay and was placed in a product-training class with ten other new hires, everyone but Patty was grateful for their new jobs. Ashamed of the lower position and boasting of her former job, she showed little respect for the instructor and found herself isolated and lonely during the training and later on the job. Patty was a victim of her own ego and inability to develop working relationships.

Use the following exercise to uncover some ways you can establish better working relationships and support in your company.

64

EXERCISE

1. Could your relationships with higher-ups use improvement? _____

   If yes, why? _____

   _____

   List three things you can do to obtain more exposure with the higher-ups:

   • _____

   • _____

   • _____

2. Could your relationship with your boss use some improvement? _____

   If yes, why? _____

   _____

   List three things you can do to gain support from your boss:

   • _____

   • _____

   • _____

3. Do you have solid relationships with your clients? _____

   If not, why not? _____

   _____

   What can you do to form a more trusting and closer bond with your clients? _____

   _____

4. Could your relationships with co-workers use some improvement? _____

If yes, why? _____

_____

List three things you can do to gain support from your co-workers:

- _____

- _____

- _____

5. Do you need to improve your relationships with workers below your job level? _____

If yes, why? _____

_____

Remember to implement these activities and develop your skills in gaining support at all levels in your organization. Do not just talk about it . . .
DO IT!

PEERS AND POWER PLAYS

Power does not always come with a position. There are many people in top company positions who have no true power. They may have authority, but that is different. Most people who are handed authority with their jobs have little or no influence in the company unless they have power. Building influence is based on performance and the cooperation of others. When people mistake power for authority, things get problematic.

You already understand the importance of peer support and peer relation-ships. What happens when these same people use the authority that goes with their positions to advance their political careers? You usually end up with power plays.

Unlike politically correct strategy, power plays usually involve very little thought. They are generally not part of a plan and are often petty. The best defense is a good offense. Politically skilled people waste little time on power plays; they use strategy and tactics when making their political moves. Power plays can be harmless in the long-run, but they are most damaging when they hurt working relationships.

Place a checkmark for each petty power play that you have been the target. Place an X in any *you* have done.

❑ Giving a false deadline for an activity

❑ Making up a rumor

❑ Complementing a person's idea when you know that it was suggested before and failed

❑ Not returning phone calls

❑ Not sharing valuable information

❑ Pretending to forget a lunch appointment with someone

❑ Controlling resources that can benefit someone else

❑ Recommending others for a project or task you know they will hate doing

❑ Agreeing to do something and not doing it

❑ Taking credit for someone else's idea

These minor power plays are hard to predict because they are usually last-minute actions of poorly skilled politicians. If you do not overreact and become defensive, you will minimize the advantage others gain. After all, one of the first things they are trying to get you to do is feel the effect and respond to it in a negative or angry manner.

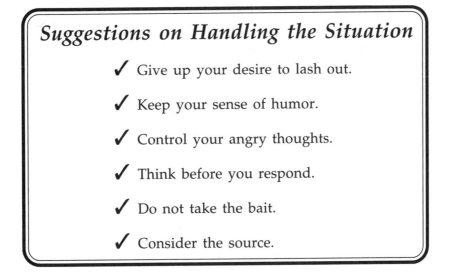

Suggestions on Handling the Situation

✓ Give up your desire to lash out.

✓ Keep your sense of humor.

✓ Control your angry thoughts.

✓ Think before you respond.

✓ Do not take the bait.

✓ Consider the source.

Awareness, maturity, and experience will become your best offensive weapons. As you become skilled in your own political crusade, the small operators will leave you alone. But if you are not there yet, keep your eyes open, for even a small spider can leave an ugly welt.

EXPLOITED WEAKNESSES

We all have weaknesses in one form or another. Some people are skilled at controlling or even hiding their "soft spots." Disclosing your weaknesses can make you vulnerable to those who would use them to advantage. This is one of the most common tactics in smear campaigns.

In a highly political organization, any political blunder you make will be someone else's gain. It is also easier to recover from a one-time blunder than a personality weakness or past mistakes.

A ruthless politician will exploit the weaknesses of those who:

- can't keep a secret
- like to gossip or lie
- have alcohol/drug problems
- are openly emotional
- lose their temper
- have relationship problems
- have something negative in their past
- have family problems
- have financial trouble
- have been fired from other jobs

Many other characteristics and behaviors can be construed as weaknesses in business. Opportunists will either uncover these or use them to their advantage once they are revealed.

You can prevent some of this from happening by simply keeping quiet about your weaknesses, personal history, and negative career experiences. To admit having a problem with depression leads to being labeled as a depressed individual. The less you tell opportunists, the less they will have to hold against you.

If your weaknesses can be improved, then do so; if not, accept them. Do not dwell on them and get on with your life. If you do not let someone else get to you, the problem maker will move on.

YOUR COMMUNICATION STYLE

You can also become characterized by your communication style. If you are defensive most of the time, you will be known for it.

Choose your words carefully in the business world and project the image you want through your communications. What you say becomes who you are in the eyes of others:

- Keep your voice firm if needed, but always speak positively and in a friendly tone.

- Know your facts and speak with confidence.

- Never attack verbally or say anything you will be ashamed of later.

- Be selective about commenting.

Political Masquerading

People who disguise who they are and their true purposes often do so to take advantage of others. Their political masquerading causes them to sometimes be referred to as "con artists." Here's how to spot them:

- ► They make attractive promises to recruit your help and offer deals that sound too good to be true.

- ► They always have success stories and let their accomplishments be known.

- ► They misrepresent their authority and are name droppers.

- ► They use guilt techniques.

- ► Though possible, their requests are usually unreasonable, and they take but rarely give back.

If you have one in your office, stay as far away as possible.

GLORY SEEKING OR HEALTHY AMBITION

Healthy ambition can be great for an individual. But in the political quest for power some people become glory seekers. Here's how to know the differences:

AMBITIOUS INDIVIDUALS	GLORY SEEKERS
• Master new skills	• Learn just enough to fake it
• Have solid friendships	• Pretend to like everyone
• Take initiative	• Go for the limelight
• Offer solutions	• Create problems
• Are team players	• Want to be the team leader
• Take risks	• Only work on a sure thing

TEAMWORK—TALENT—TENSIONS

There is a great deal of politicking that goes on in a highly competitive team environment. Some of the politics can be productive, but individual glory seekers can destroy the very principles that embody teamwork and being a team player. A valued team has:

1. A shared mission

2. A commitment to the common good of the company

3. A climate of open and free communication

4. Diversified talent and experiences

5. An environment open to creativity and risk taking

6. Flexible attitudes

7. A commitment to finding solutions

8. Individual self-direction

9. Compromise

10. Group decision making and the ability to gain consensus

Each team member should be able to accept and work within these principles. When negative politics are used by team members, the resulting conflict can disrupt the core of the project. Problem solving can become a power struggle instead of a team effort.

TEAMWORK—TALENT—TENSIONS
(continued)

If a win-lose competition creates dishonest communication and mistrust among the members, the team becomes ineffective. The process of reaching consensus on important issues is critical for the success of any team project. In order to avoid power plays and tension, teams should establish good standards:

- Ensure that members know what to expect and what is expected of them.

- Develop goals that support the project and the company.

- Define acceptable behavior and help members learn to accept as well as offer suggestions.

- Establish operating guidelines, quality standards, and productivity measures.

To refrain from practicing unethical politics, each member must fully understand the true characteristics of being a team player. Rate your skills as a team player in the following exercise.

EXERCISE

	NEVER	SOMETIMES	OFTEN	ALWAYS
1. I know how to voice my opinion on a team without creating conflict.	0	1	2	3
2. I focus on the goals of the team and my organization before considering my own gain.	0	1	2	3
3. I not only listen to others on the team, but I try to understand their point of view.	0	1	2	3
4. I work to gain agreement and use every opportunity to negotiate if things seem one-sided.	0	1	2	3
5. I do my best to help every team member use all of their skills so that we can all share in a successful project.	0	1	2	3
6. I have respect for others and I appreciate the talent each member has to offer our team.	0	1	2	3
7. I have learned how to trust my co-workers and I believe that each team member is honestly working for the good of the company.	0	1	2	3
8. I believe that everyone must be self-directed and flexible in order to work together.	0	1	2	3

Total Score _____

A perfect score of 24 makes for a fair team player.

THE TRUTH ABOUT R.E.S.P.E.C.T.

"Respect" and "politics" are often thought of as incompatible. Nothing could be further from the truth, for respect and workplace politics should go hand in hand.

Having and showing respect represents the evolution of our *relationships*, the *esteem* we place on our careers, the *style* we project, the administration of *power*, our *ethical* standards, the need to be in *control*, and the *tactics* used for an advantage. Working as a whole, they add up to *positive office politics*.

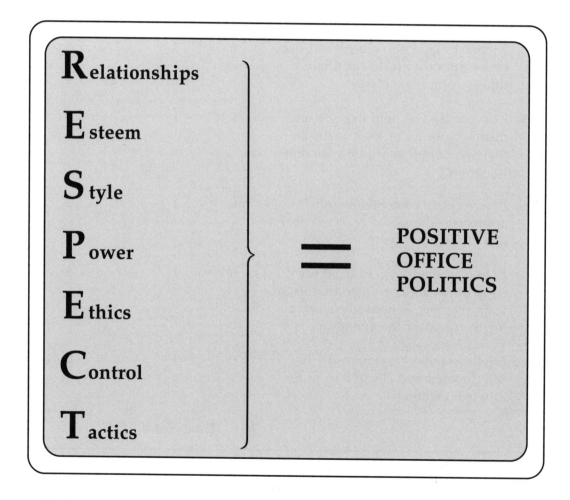

WORKPLACE FRIENDSHIPS

In business there are working relationships and friendships. But what happens when the two overlap? There is nothing wrong with having workplace friendships, but beware of *possible* complications. It is not uncommon to be competitive with and even envious of co-workers and friends. Maintaining a balance between the two kinds of relationships is vital in the workplace.

At the end of the day or a long week most friends gather to wine, dine, and play. When you are out with workplace friends, beware of "letting go" too much. It can be valuable politically to maintain a sense of professionalism at all times. This does not mean that you can't have fun, but you should always be conscious of your words and actions when out with co-workers and clients, friends or not.

Our Advice

- Act like a professional at all times and so never show disloyalty to your boss or company.

- Never say or do anything that could be held against you.

- Never agree with or comment on others' negativity if doing so can damage your reputation.

- Be a friend on matters that do not involve the office, and be an employee on issues that involve your career.

- Choose your friends carefully, and never agree to compromise your values just to prove your friendship.

- Do not give career advice if you do not want to.

> ## CASE STUDY: *A Shot at Tom*
>
> Tom was very much on the fast track with his career and began to accept more and more invitations to go out with his peers from work.
>
> One of Tom's new friends, Jim, had suggested that Tom might like to go head-to-head drinking tequila with a peer, Frank. Jim had also invited a major client to the restaurant. By the time the client arrived, Tom was not feeling so good and was quite loose-tongued.
>
> Jim had accomplished just what he intended, making Tom look bad in front of the client. You see, both Tom and Jim were being considered to handle this valuable account. Guess who got the account.

We have explored some of the ups and downs of politics in the office. Knowing that they occur doesn't help much unless you know effective strategies to enable you to succeed at office politics. Following are tips and strategies to turn you into a winner in the political arena.

SECTION

VI

The Art of Political Negotiations

*"Let us never negotiate out of fear.
But let us never fear to negotiate."*

—John F. Kennedy

NEGOTIATE WITH SKILL

In today's business world, employees at every job level must be prepared for surprises. Never assume that the people you work with will always want to cooperate. Never assume that you understand their agenda or their motives, and certainly never assume that everyone has good old-fashioned ethics.

As you strengthen your political skills, you must learn to expect the unexpected and use it to your advantage. With negotiation techniques, you can turn a surprise to your advantage, or simply use it to solve problems. Although the political goal may be to obtain the advantage, with a win–win approach your negotiation goals should be to achieve mutual agreement and satisfaction. Don't wait to negotiate until there are conflicts of interest and disagreements. The process can start long before the need. As a vital part of your political campaign, you should negotiate whenever necessary to achieve the results you desire in your personal and career goals.

Advantages to Learning Negotiation Skills

- Creating a win–win situation

- Recognizing tactics used on you

- Identifying and applying your own strategies for positioning

- Understanding the underlying factors behind conflict

- Understanding your own personal objectives and those of others

Competitive Versus Collaborative Negotiations

In politically competitive negotiation, individuals start with opposite objectives and tend to remain positional throughout the negotiation process. They often play hard and stand firm. In politically collaborative negotiation, people develop long-term working relationships. Both sides realize that the advantage of finding solutions can benefit everyone.

NEGOTIATE WITH SKILL (continued)

Your Personal Assessment and Objectives

Think about negotiation situations you have been in and answer the following questions.

1. When a co-worker or client forces a position on you, how do you usually react?

_____

_____

_____

2. If organizational conditions force you to accept an unfavorable outcome for your career, what happens the next time you have an opportunity to negotiate with your company on issues that affect you?

_____

_____

_____

3. What are your strong points in negotiation?

_____

_____

_____

4. What are your weak points that need improving?

_____

_____

_____

A Career-Saving Skill

Ask around and you will probably find that the best business leaders have not only saved their careers but advanced them with negotiation skills.

What's Important in Political Negotiations?

- Anticipating key moves

- Recognizing hidden power plays

- Knowing when to use power plays

- Anticipating risk

- Handling hostile situations

- Functioning when you are at a disadvantage

- Knowing when to lose a little to gain advantage

- Being aware of invisible promises

- Countering intimidating actions

- Preventing misunderstandings

- Spotting the con artist

- Uncovering motives

- Handling verbal and emotional abuse

- Defusing bluffs

- Handling a deadlock

- Reacting to accusations

NEGOTIABLE POLITICAL INTERESTS

When we negotiate on any issue, we should maintain a focus on interests rather than positions.

INTERESTS	POSITIONS
• Needs, wants, and concerns	• Established goals or outcomes
• Priorities among multiple needs and wants	• A fixed amount or value tied to other specified conditions
• Approximate needs and wants that can be satisfied in various ways	• A specific point to which the answer is yes or no

How to Proceed

STEP 1: Separate those who you are negotiating with from the situation. Identify the individual's interest and how it is not being met.

STEP 2: Recognize your perceptions of the situation and the emotions involved. Acknowledge emotional issues and maintain control. Use effective communication skills.

STEP 3: Define the problem and know your true interests, including which are compatible and which conflict with those of your opponent. Consider the options and stay flexible.

STEP 4: Focus on a mutual solution and remain objective. Invent new options as necessary and know what is realistically fair. Know your walk-away position.

Tips for Political Negotiations

- Encourage opponents who begin to make offers.

- Give concessions that do not destroy your position.

- Do not be afraid to say no.

- Work at gaining trust.

- Stay positive, flexible, and focused.

Hardball Negotiators

- Keep their position and insist on what they want.

- Often attack your ideas and positions.

- May use personal attacks, threats, or dirty tricks.

- May use misrepresentation or play psychological games.

- Stress tactics.

- Can have hidden agendas.

- Will test your strength.

If your opponent is playing hardball, simply stick to your agenda and continue to look for and offer solutions. In political situations, this can be difficult because the hardball player may look for every opportunity to make conditions even more difficult than they need to be. Successful negotiators keep trying to find solutions, maintain control over their emotions, and look for opportunities that will advance communications.

POLITICAL STYLES

Yes, there are different political styles, negotiation styles and, of course, personality styles. We would be unrealistic if we believed that there are only the four styles we hear about most often: consultative, avoiding, passive, and competitive. There's more to negotiations than knowing different styles.

A Look at the Dynamics of Style

No behavior represents a fixed constant. People change and their style can change often during a negotiation. An adversarial behavior can change drastically as the negotiation process develops. Keep in mind that most negotiations *do not* happen in just a few minutes or a few hours. Many can go on for days or longer.

You must remain *flexible* in your attitude in order to adjust to the many changes that can occur during the negotiation process. Yes, there are certain skills that work best with different behaviors, but you must never assume that the behavior you see at any one time will remain constant.

One very effective tactic of advanced politicians is to change style throughout the negotiating process just to confuse opponents and keep them guessing. Your own habits may end up limiting your negotiating success. If you are too predictable in your behavior and style, your opponent can gain the advantage.

How You Can Be More Effective

1. Look for shared ideas and objectives.

2. Clarify and identify the differences.

3. Gain commitment on issues that you can.

4. Accept each behavior and analyze any sudden changes in behavior.

5. Demonstrate your willingness to find a solution.

6. Respond to concerns and offer suggestions.

Remember this: If you spend too much time trying to figure out your opponent's style, you may end up behind in the game before you realize it has started. Beware of behavior, but do not let that become the focus of your negotiations. Individual style is never the issue—it is your opponent's interest you need to be concerned with.

KNOWLEDGE AND POLITICAL NEGOTIATING POWER

Knowledge, information, wisdom, and foresight can increase your political power faster than any specific negotiating "method" can. This knowledge does not come from a high IQ. It is learned and it is earned. Knowledge gives you strength in any negotiable situation. You can search out knowledge or you can gain it from experience.

Proven Negotiation Strategies That Work When You Have Information

▶ Control vital information until it can be used to your advantage. Timing is everything.

▶ When you have valuable information that is an advantage, it can be best to keep quiet.

▶ If you can act on information before your opponent knows about it, you can possibly gain the political advantage.

▶ If information you obtain leads you to develop new and innovative ideas, you may want to save those ideas and information for a greater opportunity.

▶ Ask high-gain questions at appropriate times. Others do not always volunteer information.

▶ Positioning yourself to gain valuable information is a strategy.

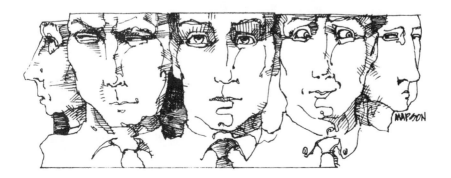

KNOWLEDGE AND POLITICAL NEGOTIATING POWER (continued)

CASE STUDY: *Tactical Advantage*

Lisa had heard from one of her clients that his company would be implementing new business procedures that would allow them to share resources, activities, and marketing ideas with their international hub in France. Although Lisa knew this information would be valuable to her boss, she said nothing to him or her co-workers, realizing that the changes would take at least a year to implement. Longing to make a career move, Lisa thought carefully and planned her strategy. She knew that one of two things would eventually happen. Either the client would need to expand with the international connection or her company would need someone positioned to handle the international side of business for that valued client.

So, Lisa spent the next year studying French and international business. When the announcement was made that both her company and the client needed someone to handle the French connection, the political ploys came from over a dozen employees. Lisa pulled her advanced knowledge out and was offered both positions. She accepted the job with the client and advanced her career and salary five years by simply investing in herself for one year. She took a risk, but it payed off and she felt she would never really lose anything by knowing French and international business.

When the Pressure Is On

Let's face it, sometimes the negotiations just don't go our way. In spite of all of our efforts, strategy, and tactics, things can go wrong and create unwelcome setbacks.

1. Do not panic
2. Consider it a challenge
3. Learn from the experience
4. Revise your plan
5. Accept criticism
6. Make a comeback
7. Focus on the positive

EXERCISE

Think about your last negotiation experience and answer the following questions:

1. How good were your skills? (Rate 1–10)

    Listening _____

    Determining motive _____

    Identifying tactics _____

    Using strategy _____

    Using counter-tactics _____

    Exchanging solutions _____

    Gaining agreement _____

2. What was the positive outcome? _____

    _____

3. Was there any negative outcome? _____

    _____

4. Do you feel it was a win–win situation? _____

    _____

5. What would you do differently next time? _____

    _____

SECTION

VII

Political Liberty

"Liberty is not a means to a higher political end. It is itself the highest political end."

—Lord Acton

YOUR POLITICAL RIGHTS

Earlier we explained briefly the pros and cons of taking the political challenge. But what are the pros and cons of political independence? True political liberty does not mean that you or your company are without politics or free of power plays. What it does mean is that within your corporate structure, you know your rights and have earned additional privileges to move more freely within known limits.

Knowing the rules and playing by the rules are two very different things for some who have earned executive privilege. This often opens the door to the following kinds of illegal abuse:

- Sexual harassment

- Blackmail

- Theft

- Fraud

- Physical and emotional abuse

- Provocation and threats

Most people will never cross the line into such behavior, but if it happens, you do have rights. Your first right is to choose if you are going to participate—whether by engaging in such abuse, accepting it in others, or being a victim of it. All are unacceptable and illegal political behavior. Even if the activity is not politically motivated, it is still not condoned in business.

If an unscrupulous individual should cause you problems as a result of such behavior, you have further rights. You should consult with a professional or inform your personnel department of such activity.

The road that leads from being controlled to being in control can be frustrating and difficult at times. Getting on the power track requires some risk, determination, and skill, but it is possible.

You can't wait for the vicious people in your life to change miraculously and you can't expect to change them. You can change yourself and take action that commands respect and decency. Be willing to take a risk, learn new skills, empower yourself, think positively not negatively, and take action.

POLITICALLY NAIVE TO POLITICALLY WISE

Those who function in a politically naive world can often get caught in the traps of others. If someone at work treats you in less than a professional manner, you could be dealing with more than just a difficult person. Some people intentionally mistreat others as a means of gaining power, control, or eliminating the competition.

There are many ways that this is done. They may not be illegal, but they certainly can be considered unethical and unacceptable. Take the test below and assess just how much you are being affected by someone else's self-serving actions.

YES   NO

1. Do you find yourself acting impatient or short-tempered at work because of tension with someone there? ❏ ❏

2. Are you losing self-confidence or second-guessing your own work because of put-downs from someone? ❏ ❏

3. Do you avoid group social invitations because a certain person could be there? ❏ ❏

4. Do you become anxious and frightened when you have to meet with a certain person at work or in a business? Do you lose sleep over it? ❏ ❏

5. Do you find yourself wondering how you could ever get on the good side with whoever is treating you badly? ❏ ❏

6. Have you considered quitting your job because of unpleasant situations at work? ❏ ❏

7. Have you passed up positive opportunities just to avoid possible conflict with someone at work? ❏ ❏

If you answered no to all of these questions, then you have a wonderful work environment or you work alone.

If you answered yes once or twice, then there is definitely a problem that should be confronted or dealt with. You could have physical and emotional problems from these uncomfortable situations.

If you answered yes three or more times, you have some serious problems to contend with. They will probably get worse if not addressed in a way that proves positive for you. Seek some professional advice and empower yourself to move forward. You should not be a victim of this behavior any longer.

THE ONLY VOTE THAT COUNTS

If you can't live with yourself because of what you inflict on others or the abuse you tolerate, then any career advance you achieve will probably be short-lived. If you are someone who mistreats or manipulates, you should assess your own behavior and develop positive ways to gain power and advance your political position. If you are someone who is being victimized, then you need to take action to put an end to it.

In any difficult situation at work, look at the history of the problem before you make any decisions or take action. There are two sides to every story. This does not mean that maltreatment is acceptable under any conditions, but it does mean that you should uncover the truth.

Not every difficulty with someone means a major problem. People often have personality clashes, or you may have caught someone having a series of bad days. Do not cry wolf every time there is a conflict. It is far more important to work out differences than to look for blame.

Take a few minutes to jot down the history surrounding a negative work situation, include your feelings, the sequence of events, and the outcome. Use it to help you sort out the truth and provide clarity to the situation. You might want to use a separate piece of paper for this valuable exercise.

_____

_____

_____

_____

_____

_____

_____

_____

_____

So how do you stay sane and productive in a cutthroat battle with a co-worker?

▶ Create strategies for taking care of yourself and keeping your emotions intact.

▶ Use effective communication skills so that you can defend yourself and your career.

▶ Develop strategies for changing the way you are being treated.

The Point of No Return

Once you decide to move forward and change the situation you are in, you can take some very important steps that are extremely beneficial.

1. Get support from a friend or colleague—someone you can trust.

2. Document the events that have led you to take action.

3. If possible, reveal the problem to an employee-relations manager or your boss, provided your boss is not the abuser.

4. Let whoever is abusing you know you will not tolerate it any longer.

5. Develop a positive plan of action.

ADDRESSING UNACCEPTABLE BEHAVIOR

All employees' unacceptable behavior should be addressed. The victim should always be listened to and any erratic behavior should be dealt with. If you ignore unacceptable behavior and don't take action, you reinforce its repetition, and send a message that threatens productivity. Early intervention is the key to defusing potentially damaging situations.

What Can Employers Do?

- Promote healthy teamwork

- Empower employees

- Be supportive and listen well

- Provide counseling for interpersonal conflict

- Handle differences effectively

- Discredit any unethical political activity

- Establish a culture of open communication

What to Watch For

These are behaviors to look for in individuals you suspect of being potentially threatening or capable of unacceptable political harassment.

- Intimidation and verbal threats, whether direct or veiled

- Paranoid behavior

- Unaccepting of criticism or help

- Holding grudges and bad-mouthing everyone

- Seeking revenge

- Obsessed with control and power

What *Not* to Do

- Cover up for an employee or make excuses for someone's behavior

- Avoid dealing with the problem or assume things will change on their own

- Go it alone and not listen to others or seek help

- Forget to keep a written record of the abuse

- Ignore the use of drugs or alcohol in the workplace

- Fail to take positive action

Outside Pressures

If you have been in business for any length of time, then chances are you have been involved in a corporate takeover, buyout, merger, joint venture, or re-engineering effort. These can threaten jobs at every level. No one is immune to fear of such uncertainty. The ethical political strategies we described earlier can often benefit those who live with such fear as well as positively affect their position. Many good employees and powerful people have been relieved of their jobs because of outside pressures. Some events cannot be changed in spite of your political efforts to come out ahead, but it is worth the try.

YOUR STRATEGY FOR SURVIVAL

1. Be prepared for anything and everything.

With eyes and ears open, you will be ready to act at the slightest change in circumstances.

► Keep up your networking and secure contacts.

► Make yourself marketable and valuable.

2. Continually sell your skills.

The new company or boss may have heard about you from others, but you must be prepared to convince them of your value and talent.

► Position yourself to be heard, prove your worth, show how you will fit in, and create a need for yourself.

► Know the structure and learn about new developments.

3. Take a positive approach and attitude toward change.

Flexibility could determine whether you survive changes within your cooperation.

► Show your support for new opportunity.

► Be careful not to voice complaints to others.

► Show you can adapt and be agreeable.

Plan B

If you do not survive the cuts and can't remain with your company, you should take the following steps:

- Call in any favors from previous politicking and contacts.

- Be flexible in your career abilities.

- Contact employment recruiters.

- Be willing to do consulting work; it could result in a full-time job.

- Never bad-mouth the old company or new arrangement; you could be called back.

IT'S NOT WHETHER YOU WIN OR LOSE . . . OR IS IT?

As you move forward with your new political knowledge, remember that correct and effective politics should not be a battle of strength and determination. It is neither a means of conflict resolution, nor a method to feed egos. But it is about "power," the most desired and misunderstood factor in business. Political knowledge is also about getting and maintaining advantage throughout your career. It is not political strategy, power, or advantage that will make you a winner in life and in business; it is the way you use them.

Talent, energy, skill, attitude, and determination come from within. These are the things that champions are made of. The transition from average employee to company hero isn't easy. Personal pride and patience can often be a foundation on which to build, but hard work, honesty, and development will cause you to advance.

Never take the challenge just to beat out others. Challenge yourself and find the excitement and rewards of a lifetime that lie ahead.

Good Luck!

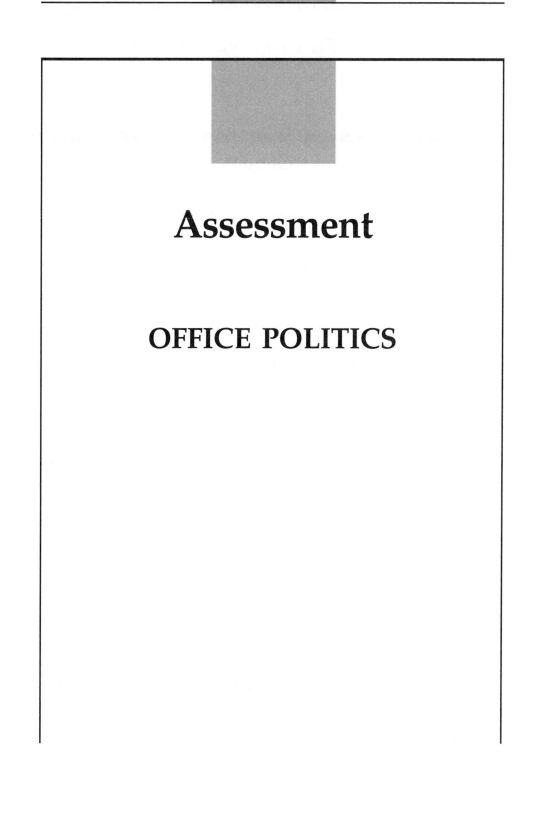

Assessment

OFFICE POLITICS

OFFICE POLITICS
POSITIVE RESULTS FROM FAIR PRACTICES

A FIFTY-MINUTE™ BOOK

The objectives of this book are:

1. to discuss the need for being political in the workplace.

2. to explain positive political techniques.

3. to explain strategies of political negotiating.

4. to discuss negative politics and to show how to deal with them.

OBJECTIVE ASSESSMENT FOR OFFICE POLITICS

Select the best response.

1. Political situations are
   A. have only recently become a part of business.
   B. uncommon in today's workplace.
   C. common in today's workplace.
   D. present in government agencies only.

2. Business communication suffers from workplace politics.
   A. True
   B. False

3. A good political career move is to
   A. appear affluent.
   B. avoid being a workplace leader.
   C. build solid workplace relationships.
   D. all of the above.
   E. B and C.

4. In furthering your career, you should work for
   A. being a champion in whatever way works.
   B. holding tight and not conceding.
   C. seeking win-win situations.
   D. personal power.

5. When faced with gossip and rumors, your best reaction is to
   A. stay silent and aware.
   B. contribute what you know.
   C. realize that all gossip is false.
   D. all of the above.
   E. A and B.

6. Those who avoid being political at work
   A. run the risk of being isolated.
   B. may not move forward in their careers.
   C. may find themselves frustrated and resentful.
   D. all of the above.
   E. A and C.

OBJECTIVE ASSESSMENT (continued)

7. Are any of these political activities unethical?
   a. leaving nothing to chance.
   b. cultivating relationships with higher ranking people.
   c. developing followers.
   A. yes
   B. no

8. Power can
   A. disadvantage some people.
   B. maximize performance.
   C. help others.
   D. all of the above.
   E. B and C.

Read the following case study and then answer the questions that follow.

As a government employee, Al finds that procedures change every time a new boss is elected. As an old-timer, he believes that the procedures endorsed by his newest boss will be less efficient than those already in place.

9. If Al just does as he is told, he will probably
   A. enjoy his job more.
   B. enjoy his job less.
   C. avoid stress temporarily.
   D. A and C.
   E. B and C.

10. If Al decides to discuss the situation with his boss, he will be
    A. engaging in office politics.
    B. taking a risk.
    C. accepting stress temporarily.
    D. all of the above.
    E. B and C.

Select the best response.

11. High-level politically driven decisions are seldom completely clear to all those involved.
    A. True
    B. False

12. To be politically wise, you should
    A. focus on the facts.
    B. understand the options.
    C. insist on total understanding.
    D. all of the above.
    E. A and B.

13. If you compromise your values and ethics, you may
    A. get what you want.
    B. lose the trust of those with influence.
    C. both of the above.

14. Power-hungry people who violate human rights
    A. can be successful.
    B. are not successful.
    C. often self-destruct.
    D. never act deviously.
    E. A and C.

15. The best solution to blackmail, stealing ideas, or back stabbing at work is
    A. changing jobs.
    B. isolating yourself.
    B. opening up communication.
    B. giving back the same tactic.

16. If a person in authority is out to get rid of you, a good tactic would be to
    A. establish allies.
    B. attack the attacker.
    C. close off your vulnerabilities.
    D. all of the above.
    E. A and C.

17. Personal support in the workplace is
    A. unnecessary if you prefer to work alone.
    B. necessary at all levels.
    C. necessary only with customers.

18. Authority always means power.
    A. True
    B. False

19. If you have a weakness such as family problems or depression, your best action in the workplace is to
    A. be open and honest about it.
    B. usually keep quiet about it.
    C. avoid revealing it to opportunists.
    D. A and C.
    E. B and C.

OBJECTIVE ASSESSMENT (continued)

20. Healthy ambition involves
    A. going for the limelight.
    B. taking initiative.
    C. being a team player.
    D. all of the above.
    E. B and C.

21. A good team player
    A. clarifies expectations.
    B. supports learning and creativity.
    C. works for wise consensus.
    D. is flexible.
    E. all of the above.

22. If your friends are from your workplace, you should avoid
    A. seeing them outside of work.
    B. compromising your career.
    C. disloyalty to your boss or your friends.
    D. B and C.
    E. A and C.

23. When working with a group, you can assume that
    A. everyone is willing to cooperate.
    B. you will understand everyone's motives.
    C. negotiation will proceed smoothly.
    D. all of the above.
    E. none of the above.

24. Your political power can benefit most from
    A. skilled negotiating strategies.
    B. information, knowledge and foresight.

25. To survive in today's workplace, you should
    A. be prepared for anything.
    B. sharpen your skills.
    C. be positive about change.
    D. create a need for yourself.
    E. all of the above.

Qualitative Objectives for *Office Politics*

To discuss the need for being political in the workplace:

Questions 1, 6, 9, 17, 18, 25

To explain positive political techniques:

Questions 3, 8, 10, 20, 21, 22

To explain strategies of political negotiating:

Questions 4, 7, 11, 12, 13, 21, 23, 24

To discuss negative politics and to show how to deal with them:

Questions 2, 5, 14, 15, 16, 19

ANSWER KEY

1. C	**10.** D	**18.** B
2. A	**11.** A	**19.** E
3. C	**12.** E	**20.** E
4. C	**13.** C	**21.** E
5. A	**14.** E	**22.** D
6. D	**15.** C	**23.** E
7. B	**16.** E	**24.** B
8. D	**17.** B	**25.** E
9. E		

NOTES

NOTES

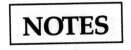

NOTES

NOW AVAILABLE FROM CRISP PUBLICATIONS

Books • Videos • CD Roms • Computer-Based Training Products

If you enjoyed this book, we have great news for you. There are over 200 books available in the *50-Minute*™ Series. To request a free full-line catalog, contact your local distributor or Crisp Publications, Inc., 1200 Hamilton Court, Menlo Park, CA 94025. Our toll-free number is 800-442-7477.

Subject Areas Include:

Management

Human Resources

Communication Skills

Personal Development

Marketing/Sales

Organizational Development

Customer Service/Quality

Computer Skills

Small Business and Entrepreneurship

Adult Literacy and Learning

Life Planning and Retirement

CRISP WORLDWIDE DISTRIBUTION

English language books are distributed worldwide. Major international distributors include:

ASIA/PACIFIC

Australia/New Zealand: In Learning, PO Box 1051 Springwood QLD, Brisbane, Australia 4127
Telephone: 7-3841-1061, Facsimile: 7-3841-1580   ATTN: Messrs. Gordon

Singapore: Graham Brash (Pvt) Ltd. 32, Gul Drive, Singapore 2262
Telephone: 65-861-1336, Facsimile: 65-861-4815   ATTN: Mr. Campbell

CANADA

Reid Publishing, Ltd., Box 69559-109 Thomas Street, Oakville,
Ontario Canada L6J 7R4.
Telephone: (905) 842-4428, Facsimile: (905) 842-9327   ATTN: Mr. Reid

Trade Book Stores: Raincoast Books, 8680 Cambie Street,
Vancouver, British Columbia, Canada V6P 6M9.
Telephone: (604) 323–7100, Facsimile: 604-323-2600   ATTN: Ms. Laidley

EUROPEAN UNION

England: Flex Training, Ltd. 9-15 Hitchin Street, Baldock,
Hertfordshire, SG7 6A, England
Telephone: 1-462-896000, Facsimile: 1-462-892417   ATTN: Mr. Willetts

INDIA

Multi-Media HRD, Pvt., Ltd., National House, Tulloch Road, Appolo Bunder,
Bombay, India 400-039
Telephone: 91-22-204-2281, Facsimile: 91-22-283-6478   ATTN: Messrs. Aggarwal

MIDDLE EAST

United Arab Emirates: Al-Mutanabbi Bookshop, PO Box 71946, Abu Dhabi
Telephone: 971-2-321-519, Facsimile: 971-2-317-706   ATTN: Mr. Salabbai

SOUTH AMERICA

Mexico: Grupo Editorial Iberoamerica, Serapio Rendon #125, Col. San Rafael,
06470 Mexico, D.F.
Telephone: 525-705-0585, Facsimile: 525-535-2009   ATTN: Señor Grepe

SOUTH AFRICA

Alternative Books, Unit A3 Sanlam Micro Industrial Park, Hammer Avenue
STRYDOM Park, Randburg, 2194 South Africa
Telephone: 2711 792 7730, Facsimile: 2711 792 7787   ATTN: Mr. de Haas